The Holy Ghost Is like a Blanket

Written by **Annalisa Hall**

Illustrated by **Corey Egbert**

CFI

An Imprint of Cedar Fort, Inc.

Springville, Utah

Who is
the Holy Ghost?

What is He like?

He is a member of
the Godhead.

The Holy Ghost is like a dove.

A dove is gentle and rests in peaceful places. The still, small voice of the Holy Ghost is gentle and quiet too. The Holy Ghost will descend slowly while you are reverent and peaceful.

He is like a dove. What else?

The Holy Ghost is like the wind.
You can feel and hear the wind's power.
But like the Holy Ghost, you cannot
see the wind as it whispers and
whistles. You can feel the Holy
Ghost in your heart as He warns
you of danger and helps
you choose the right.

He is like the wind.
What else?

The Holy Ghost is like glasses.

When someone cannot see well, things are fuzzy and confusing. Like a pair of glasses, the Holy Ghost helps you to see things clearly so you can make good choices.

He is like glasses. What else?

The Holy Ghost is like a book.

A book uses words and pictures to teach. When you ask for help, the Holy Ghost helps you remember what to say and do. The Holy Ghost teaches truth anytime and anywhere. Most important, He testifies of Heavenly Father and Jesus Christ.

He is like a book. What else?

The Holy Ghost is like a flashlight.

A flashlight shines brightly in the darkness. The Holy Ghost fills darkness with light. He brightens your heart and mind. The light of the Holy Ghost shines best when you choose to live the gospel.

The Holy Ghost is like a hug.

A hug is friendly, kind, and loving. The Holy Ghost can be your friend as you are kind to others. The warm friendship of the Holy Ghost makes you happy.

He is like a hug.
What else?

The Holy Ghost is like a star.

A star is steady, is always there, and leads you on the right path. The Holy Ghost hopes you will seek His help. He is ready to guide you back to Heavenly Father.

He is like a star.
What else?

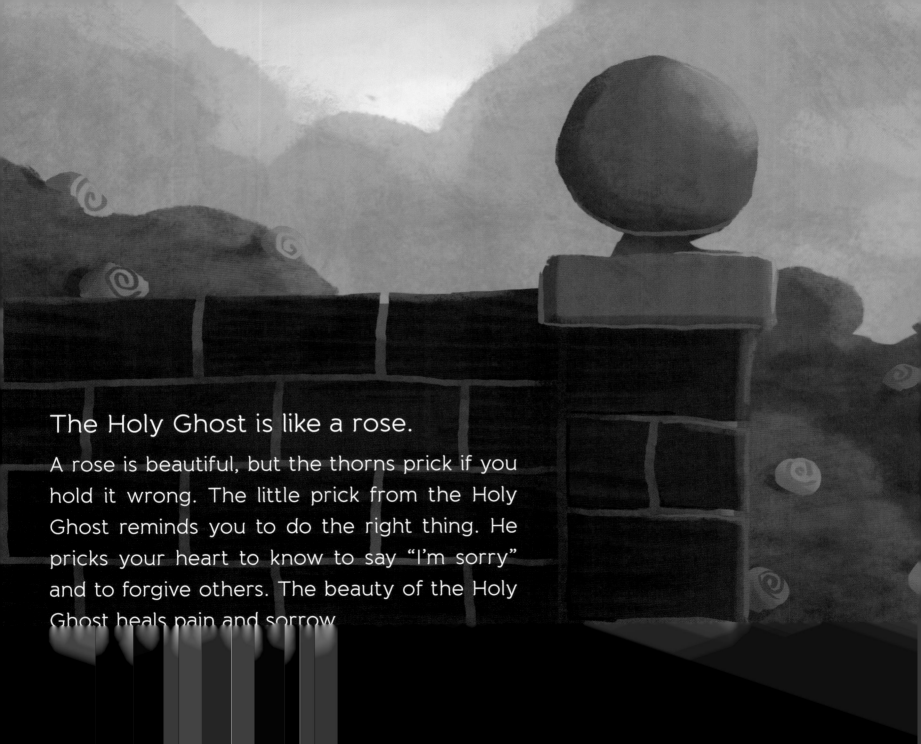

The Holy Ghost is like a rose.

A rose is beautiful, but the thorns prick if you hold it wrong. The little prick from the Holy Ghost reminds you to do the right thing. He pricks your heart to know to say "I'm sorry" and to forgive others. The beauty of the Holy Ghost heals pain and sorrow.

He is like a rose. What else?

The Holy Ghost is like a seashell.

When you put a seashell next to your ear, you can hear a light humming. The different whispers of the Holy Ghost speak to your heart, mind, and soul. If you're not paying attention, you cannot hear what the Holy Ghost has to say to you.

He is like a seashell.
What else?

The Holy Ghost is like a train.

A train carries things and travels great distances. The Holy Ghost is a vehicle of revelation. He carries messages to you from Heavenly Father. He brings good people into your life. He travels with you.

He is like a train. What else?

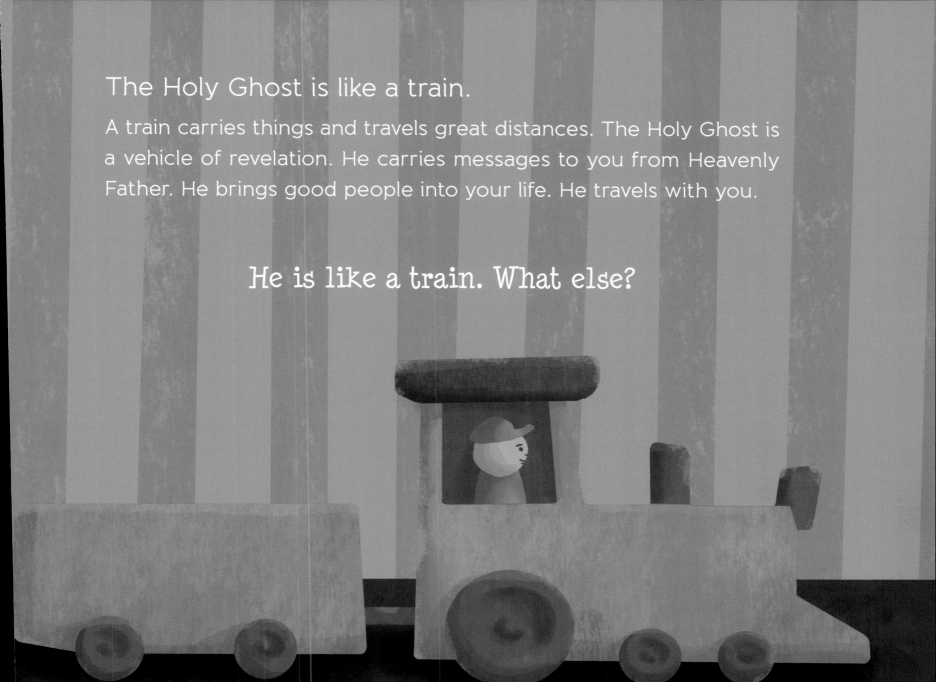

The Holy Ghost is like an umbrella.

The umbrella shields you from a storm. Like the umbrella, the Holy Ghost gives you courage and confidence to go forward. By obedience to the Holy Ghost's promptings, you are safe and secure.

He is like an umbrella.

What else?

The Holy Ghost is like a blanket.

He is a special gift from Heavenly Father to comfort you. The Holy Ghost wraps you in a warm and comforting feeling when you are sad or need a friend.

The Holy Ghost is like a blanket
of comfort for me.

The End

THE HOLY GHOST IS LIKE A DOVE

"He saw the heavens opened, and the Spirit like a dove descending upon him." (Mark 1:10)

"I saw a pillar of light exactly over my head, above the brightness of the sun, which descended gradually until it fell upon me." (Joseph Smith—History 1:16)

"I Want to be Reverent" (*Children's Songbook*, 28a)

THE HOLY GHOST IS LIKE THE WIND

"For thus it whispereth me, according to the workings of the Spirit of the Lord which is in me." (Words of Mormon 1:7)

"You shall feel that it is right." (Doctrine & Covenants 9:8)

"God's Love" (*Children's Songbook*, 97)

THE HOLY GHOST IS LIKE GLASSES

"By the power of the Spirit our eyes were opened and our understandings were enlightened, so as to see and understand the things of God—" (Doctrine & Covenants 76:12)

"Blessed are the eyes which see the things that ye see." (Luke 10:23)

"The Still Small Voice" (*Children's Songbook*, 106)

THE HOLY GHOST IS LIKE A BOOK

"And by the power of the Holy Ghost ye may know the truth of all things." (Moroni 10:5)

"Holy Ghost beareth record of the Father and me." (3 Nephi 28:11)

"Search, Ponder, and Pray" (*Children's Songbook*, 109)

THE HOLY GHOST IS LIKE A FLASHLIGHT

"The light and the life of the world; a light which shineth in darkness and the darkness comprehendeth it not." (Doctrine & Covenants 39:2)

"Then I saw that wisdom excelleth folly, as far as light excelleth darkness." (Ecclesiastes 2:13)

"Teach Me To Walk In the Light" (*Hymns*, 304; *Children's Songbook*, 117)

THE HOLY GHOST IS LIKE A HUG

"They are encircled about with the matchless bounty of his love." (Alma 26:15)

"Fruit of the Spirit is love, joy, peace." (Galatians 5:22)

"I Feel My Savior's Love" (*Children's Songbook*, 74)

THE HOLY GHOST IS LIKE A STAR

"Thou hast been enlightened by the Spirit of truth."
(Doctrine & Covenants 6:15)

"Put your trust in that Spirit which leadeth to do good."
(Doctrine & Covenants 11:12)

"Beautiful Savior" (*Children's Songbook*, 62)

THE HOLY GHOST IS LIKE A ROSE

"They were pricked in their heart." (Acts 2:37)

"Know we the spirit of truth, and the spirit of error."
(1 John 4:6)

"Choose the Right Way" (*Children's Songbook*, 160)

THE HOLY GHOST IS LIKE A SEASHELL

"Hearken, O ye people, and open your hearts and give
ear from afar; and listen." (Doctrine & Covenants 63:1)

"All my words that I shall speak unto thee receive in
thine heart, and hear with thine ears." (Ezekiel 3:10)

"Listen, Listen (Round)" (*Children's Songbook*, 107)

THE HOLY GHOST IS LIKE A TRAIN

"And it came to pass that after I, Nephi, had been
carried away in the spirit, and seen all these things,
I returned to the tent of my father." (1 Nephi 15:1)

"And he came by the Spirit into the temple." (Luke 2:27)

"Nearer My God to Thee" (*Hymns*, 100)

THE HOLY GHOST IS LIKE AN UMBRELLA

"Thou hast also given me the shield of thy salvation:
and thy gentleness hath made me great."
(2 Samuel 22:36)

"In quietness and confidence shall be your strength."
(Isaiah 30:15)

"When I Am Baptized" (*Children's Songbook*, 103)

THE HOLY GHOST IS LIKE A BLANKET

"Wherefore, I now send upon you another Comforter,
even upon you my friends, that it may abide in your
hearts, even the Holy Spirit of promise; which other
Comforter is the same that I promised unto my
disciples, as is recorded in the testimony of John."
(Doctrine & Covenants 88:3)

"The Holy Ghost" (*Children's Songbook*, 105)

For Geoff, Linc, Hari, Marle & you

—Annalisa Hall

For Mom, Dad, Sarah, Oliver, Rex &
especially Natalya. You've made me who I am.
I love you!

—Corey Egbert

Text © 2013, 2018 Annalisa Hall
Illustrations © 2018 Corey Egbert

ISBN 13: 978-1-4621-2244-8

Published by CFI, an imprint of Cedar Fort, Inc.
2373 W. 700 S., Springville, UT 84663
Distributed by Cedar Fort, Inc. www.cedarfort.com

The Library of Congress has cataloged the Girls' edition as follows:

Hall, Annalisa, 1978- author.
The Holy Ghost is like a blanket / Annalisa Hall.
pages cm
ISBN 978-1-4621-1229-6
1. Holy Spirit--Juvenile literature. 2. Mormon children--Religious life--Juvenile literature. 3. Gift of the Holy Ghost (Mormon theology)--Juvenile literature. I. Egbert, Corey, 1988- illustrator. II. Title.

BX8643.H63H35 2013
231'.3--dc23

2013002263

Cover and interior layout design by Shawnda T. Craig
Cover design © 2018 Cedar Fort, Inc.
Edited by Catherine M. Christensen and Emily S. Chambers

Printed in the United States of America

10 9 8 7 6 5 4 3 2 1